Moments for Fabulous Fathers

Written by
Robert J. Strand

ORDERING INFORMATION
Individual sales can be had at selected bookstores or you can order direct from Rojon, Inc. at P.O. Box 3898, Springfield, MO 65808-3898 or call our customer service number, 888-389-0225.
Quantity sales are available at special discounts on bulk purchases by corporations, associations, churches and others. For details, contact Rojon Inc. at the above address.
Orders by trade bookstores and wholesalers can be made through the above address as well.

ISBN: 0-9717039-1-4

Third printing: February 2004

All Scripture references are from **"The New King James Version"** (Thomas Nelson Publishers) unless otherwise noted.

Design by Marc Mcbride

ROJON PUBLISHING
P. O. Box 3898
Springfield, MO 65808-3898
Fax: 417-883-0556

Presented to:

_____

Presented by:

_____

Date:

_____

Dedication:

To the fathers in my life who have given me understanding and insight into fatherhood. They are my deceased father, John; deceased father-in-law, Leo; two sons who are now fathers, Marc and Kirk; and son-in-law, Eric.
Thanks for the life lessons!

Contents

Love

THE late Grady Nutt, humorist, speaker, motivator, told this story about a young family who had invited their new pastor and his spouse over for a special Sunday dinner.

The mother of the house was determined and concerned that it be a "perfect" affair. Everything must be just right so as to make a good impression. So she drilled their two children days in advance about the proper behavior, which fork to use when, how to spread a napkin, what to say and what not to do.

Finally, the special Sunday arrived. The meal had been cooked to perfection. It was timed and ready to be served at the announced time. Everyone was invited to come into the dining room where the table had been set with a beautiful white tablecloth, the best china, good silverware, floral centerpiece, candles, place cards...everything to make it the perfect dinner.

When the blessing had been pronounced by the father, their nine-year-old daughter reached for her glass of iced tea and knocked it over! The little brother jumped up to get out of the way of the spreading stain and knocked his glass of tea over, too!

An awkward moment of silence followed as everyone looked at the mother, realizing how disappointed she must be. She had gone through so much preparation and extra work to make this a wonderful meal...and now there was a huge widening stain of tea and ice cubes in the middle of her best white linen table cloth – one that had come from Ireland.

But...before anybody could say anything, the father flipped over his own glass of tea and started to laugh. The preacher quickly caught on...he tipped his tea over and began to laugh, too! The preacher's wife then knocked over her glass and joined the laughter.

Then everyone looked to the mother. Finally, after a pause, with an expression of resignation, she picked up her glass and just dumped it out in the middle of the table. Everybody around the table roared with laughter.

THEN...the father looked down at his nine-year-old daughter sitting next to him. And, he winked at her. As she laughed, embarrassingly, she looked up at her father and winked back. But as she did, her eyelash flicked a tear out onto her cheek and it rolled down her face. She was looking, almost worshipfully, at a father who loved her enough to be sensitive to save her from one of life's most embarrassing moments.

To be a father requires love...first and foremost. And this love is an action directed to another person or persons, an action which is motivated by caring and it is given freely, without any thought of personal reward in mind.

And above all things have fervent love for one another, for "love will cover a multitude of sins." Be hospitable to one another without grumbling.
(I Peter 4:8-9)

Perseverance

IT WAS MONDAY NIGHT, August third, at the 1992 Olympics in Barcelona, Spain. At the track and field stadium, the gun sounded for the 400 meter semi-finals.

About 100 meters into the race, Great Britain's Derek Redmond crumpled to the track with a torn right hamstring.

Medical attendants rushed to assist him but as they approached Redmond, he waved them all aside. He struggled to his feet, stumbled and hopped in a desperate effort to finish the race. At times he was on all fours crawling toward the finish line.

Four years earlier he had also qualified for the 1988 Olympics in Seoul, Korea. Ninety seconds before his heat he had to pull out of the race because of an achilles tendon problem. Following this injury he had five surgeries. Yet, somehow he had qualified again for the 1992 Olympics and this event...and now, he'd just suffered a career-ending injury!

But he said to himself, "I'm not quitting! Somehow, I'm going to finish this race!" Painfully he worked his way toward the finish. The stands were hushed, captured by the drama they were seeing unfold before their eyes. It was agony just to watch the struggle.

Up in the stands, a huge guy wearing a T-shirt, tennis shoes and a Nike cap that said, "JUST DO IT" across the front came barreling out of the stands, hurled aside a security guard, jumped the barrier, ran to Derek Redmond's side and embraced him. He was Jim Redmond, Derek's father!

Jim was one of those sports dads who changed his whole life for the sake of his athlete child. He changed jobs. He moved to find the best training coach and setting for his son.

Now…arm around his son's waist, Derek's arm around his dad's thick shoulders and neck, they continued down the track. The crowd is stunned and now on its feet applauding. Back home his sister, who was pregnant, went into false labor. Mom is weeping in the stands. There at the stadium the crowd is standing, cheering and weeping! Derek and his dad work their way around the track until…finally, painfully, they cross the finish line, together!

Later when interviewed by the press, Jim Redmond said, "We had an agreement he was going to finish the race. This was his last Olympics. He trained eight years for this day. I wasn't going to not let him finish!"

If this is the way an earthly father responds to his son who is determined to finish his race, no matter the price, how much more does God, our Heavenly Father, come to the side and help the son or daughter who says, "I'm finishing my race!"

Listen to Me…all you, you whom I have upheld since you were conceived and have carried since your birth. Even to your old age and gray hairs I am He, I am He who will sustain you! I have made you and I will carry you; I will sustain you and I will rescue you! (Isaiah 46:3-4)

Fathering

THE FOLLOWING is a compilation of quotes about dad taken from a group of elementary kids. They were asked to complete the sentence, "A dad is good for…" Let's take a look.

A DAD IS GOOD FOR…

A dad is good for putting worms on a hook when you go fishing.

A dad is good for helping you learn to ride a two wheel bike because he can run alongside and catch you when you fall.

A dad is good for telling your aunt you don't want her to kiss you in public kind of places.

A dad is good for helping you with your homework for about two years after your mom has given up.

A dad is good for explaining to your mom why it's not such a huge crime to tear your pants sliding into second base.

A dad is good for fixing your wagon and your bike and your race car set.

A dad is good for letting you run the power mower while your mom is sitting on the porch praying.

A dad is good for teaching you how to play catch.

A dad is good for telling you the meaning of words you're too embarrassed to ask your mom about.

A dad is good for explaining to your mom why you want to get a drum set instead of taking violin lessons.

A dad is good for carrying you when you are tired and your mom won't stop shopping.

A dad is good for holding you up so you don't get water up your nose when you're trying to learn how to swim.

A dad is good for chauffeuring you where you want to go, especially if you can teach him not to talk much after you're 13 and your friends are in the car.

A dad is good for teaching you how to drive a car when you get old enough to drive.

A dad is good for helping your mom understand why you can't be clean all the time or your room can't be picked up all the time.

A dad is good to have because without him life would be frightening.

Life is sort of like the game of tennis…the player who serves well seldom loses!

**"But he who is greatest among you shall
be your servant."
(Matthew 23:11)**

Give Us Men

GOD give us men.
A time like this demands
Strong minds, great hearts,
true faith
and ready hands!

Men whom the lust of office
does not kill,
Men whom the spoils of office
cannot buy,
Men who possess opinions and a will,
Men who love honor,
Men who cannot lie.

(Josiah Gilbert Holland)

Focus

THERE IS AN INTERESTING STORY behind the first ever hole-in-one on the 12th hole at Augusta, Georgia during the fabled "Master's Tournament." It happened like this:

Claude Harmon and Ben Hogan were paired together for the third round of this particular day. While the two were good friends, their personalities were worlds apart. Harmon was outgoing and charismatic. Hogan, on the other hand, was always professional and business-like, always focused, especially on the golf course.

Harmon had the honors as they came to the twelfth tee. He promptly stepped up to the tee and knocked the ball into the cup for the first ever hole-in-one during the Master's. The crowd went wild!

Hogan, however, did not say a word to Harmon. No congratulatory shake of the hand, no tip of the hat, no acknowledgment of any kind. He simply stepped up to the ball in his business-like manner and hit a great tee shot which dropped within six feet of the cup on the twelfth.

As the two players made their way from the tee to the green, the crowd again roared and applauded for Harmon. When he retrieved his ball from the cup, once again, the crowd went wild. All this, while Hogan was in deep concentration, seemingly oblivious to the historic event he had just witnessed. He surveyed his putt, read the green, and in typical Hogan manner, stroked the ball into the cup for a birdie!

As they made their way to the 13th tee, the crowd was still buzzing from Harmon's feat. Hogan finally spoke up. He said, "You know, Claude, that is the first '2' I've ever made on that hole."

Is there a life lesson to be learned from Hogan? Yes. It's so easy to get caught

up in the accomplishments of others that we fail to focus on our own potential and future. We can be side-tracked so easily and miss what we can be capable of achieving.

Now a question for you: "If Ben Hogan had become caught up in the excitement of that hole-in-one...do you think he would have been able to keep focused enough to make his own birdie?" Interesting to think about.

Keep focused on the important...don't let anything come between you and your goals!

People will judge you by your actions and the goals you achieve, not your intentions. You might have a heart of gold as well as golden goals...but so does a hard-boiled egg.

"One thing I do, forgetting those things which are behind and reaching forward to those things which are ahead, I press toward the goal for the prize..." (Philippians 3:13b-14a)

Finish Line

A SMALL CONTROVERSY arose at the *USA/Mobil Indoor Track and Field Championships* which were being held in New York City.

The men's mile was declared a dead heat in 3 minutes and 57.35 seconds (3:57.35) between Steve Scott and Marcus O'Sullivan. Both runners agreed that Scott, with a late surge and lean, had reached the finish line tape slightly ahead of O'Sullivan. Scott even took a victory lap.

He should have known better. Finish line tapes for track events are always a few inches beyond the real finish line so that they don't interfere with the electronic photo timer, which sits at the actual finish line.

"I feel a little cheated," said Scott. "What's the point of having a finish line tape if it's not where the finish-line is?" But as Bob Hersh, rules committee chairman of the "Athletics Congress," track's U.S.A. governing body, says, "Indoors there's a lot of clutter and different finish lines are used for different races. The tape provides a visual clue for fans and runners."

Then, when asked how Scott, a veteran miler, could not know exactly where to finish, Hersh replied, "The fact is, most athletes don't read the rule book. They just show up and run."

Let's talk about that a bit more. Do you have a real finish line in sight? Have you read the rule book lately? May I suggest the following as you move to your finish line?

1) FALL FORWARD! Everybody at some time or other stumbles on his way to the finish line. Sometimes we do fall over big or little obstacles. When you fall...fall forward toward your goal!

2) GET UP WHEN YOU FALL DOWN!   Not only physically but mentally and spiritually as well. Don't just lie there, get up! Get going, start all over again. The disgrace is in staying down.

3) WHEN YOU FALL DOWN, DON'T GET UP EMPTY HANDED! If you gain something for the race of life every time you fall, even when you lose…you still win!

These three simple steps of learning how to win even if you fall are a time proven method for failing your way to successful living. Therefore, why be fearful of failing when you know that even in failure you can be a winner?!

Go for it! Reach for the tape! Lean into your goal!

IF YOU REACH FOR THE STARS AND COME UP SHORT…YOU MAY BE HUMAN. BUT YOU WILL BE DIFFERENT FROM THOSE WHO HAVE NEVER TRIED.

THEREFORE we also, since we are surrounded by so great a cloud of witnesses, let us lay aside every weight and the sin which so easily ensnares us and let us run with endurance the race that is set before us, looking unto Jesus, the author and finisher of our faith…
(Hebrews 12:1-2a)

Understanding

JOE GORDON was one of the greatest second basemen in major league history. It was during his prime, in 1947, when he was playing for the Cleveland Indians. Joe was having a great season.

And during this season, a young African American athlete named Larry Doby was signed to play for the Indians...the first black rookie to join an American League baseball team. It was history in the making.

Of course, Doby was tense and nervous as he stepped into the batter's box for the first time at bat in the major leagues. The first pitch, he swung and missed it a foot...the second pitch and again he missed it badly. The third pitch, the crowd is buzzing, and he missed it again, about a foot high in his swing.

Doby walked back to the dugout with his head down, not looking at anybody in the dugout or in the stands. He walked past every other Cleveland player on the bench, slumped down on the bench in a corner all by himself, alone, head down and in his hands just staring at the floor in dejection.

Joe Gordon, a power hitter, was the next man up. The opposing pitcher was one that Gordon practically owned and usually hit him all over the ball park and some outside of the park. But this time he stepped into the batters box and took a wild swing at the first three pitches...missing them by at least a foot and half to two feet. The crowd was puzzled and buzzing as Joe returned to the dugout, head down, not talking or looking at any of his teammates. He walked past every other player on the bench, sat down in the corner right next to Doby and put his head in his hands.

No one ever asked Gordon if he had deliberately struck out that day. But, in every ball game after that, as long as they played together, each time that Doby took his place out on the field...he always, first thing, picked up Gordon's glove and

tossed it to him with a smile of thanks. And the rest is now baseball history. Larry Doby went on to become one of the best and strongest hitters in the major leagues. He also said that Gordon's relationship with him was one of the main reasons why his career became so successful.

Now the question: Do you think Joe Gordon's act of understanding made the difference? Makes you wonder just how much more successful he became because of this. There's another observation…Gordon didn't say a word, at least not at this time. He put it into an action which could be easily understood by all who were part of the team. What a man!

Nobody will know what you mean by saying that "God is love" unless you act it as well.

(Lawrence P. Jacks)

A word fitly spoken is like apples of gold in settings of silver.
(Proverbs 25:11)

Preparation

THE FOLLOWING is supposedly taken from the U. S. Government Peace Corps Manual written for use by its volunteers who work in the jungles of the Amazon. It has instructions on what to do in case you are attacked by an "anaconda." Now…if you don't know, an "anaconda" is the world's largest snake. It's a relative to the boa constrictor but the anaconda can grow to thirty-five feet in length and can weigh between three to four hundred pounds at this size.

THIS IS WHAT THE MANUAL SAID:

1) If you are attacked by an anaconda, do not run. The snake is faster than you are.

2) Lie flat on the ground. Put your arms tight against your sides, your legs tight against one another.

3) Tuck your chin in.

4) The snake will come and begin to nudge and climb over your body.

5) Do not panic. (Now, just think about that…**DO NOT PANIC!** Oh, sure we'll be calm!)

6) After the snake has examined you, it will begin to swallow you from the feet end…always from the feet end. Permit the snake to swallow your feet and ankles. Do not panic.

7) The snake will now begin to suck your legs into its body. You must lie perfectly still. This will take a long time.

8) When the snake has reached your knees, slowly, and with as little movement as possible, reach down, take your knife and very gently slide it into the side of the snake's mouth between the edge of its mouth and your leg. Then suddenly rip upwards, severing the snake's head.

(These last two suggestions are really something else!)

9) Be sure you have a knife.

10) Be sure your knife is sharp.

Awesome! Not a pretty picture and not something I'm very eager to enjoy. And like so many government manuals…laughable. But there's a kernel of truth lodged here, too. Preparation requires just that, to prepare is to take actions for any need or problem in advance of facing the actual problem. One of the major responsibilities of fathers is the life preparation of little ones entrusted to our care. There are all kinds of snakes out there in the world waiting to devour the innocent. Our adversary, the devil, is also called a "serpent" as well as an "angel of light." Good preparation includes weapons that are sharp and instructions that are clear.

In 1976, the Indiana Hoosiers basketball team was undefeated and captured the NCAA National Championship under Bobby Knight's leadership. He was interviewed on "60 Minutes" and asked, "Why is it, Bobby, that your basketball teams at Indiana are always so successful? Is it the will to succeed?"
*"The will to succeed is important," replied Knight, "but I'll tell you what's more important…**IT'S THE WILL TO PREPARE.** It's the will to go out there every day, training and building those muscles and sharpening those skills."*

For we are His workmanship, created in Christ Jesus for good works, which God prepared beforehand that we should walk in them.
(Ephesians 2:11)

Risk

J. G. ROSCO earned multiplied millions of dollars at the height of the stock market during the 1920s. But he had a dream. In 1929, just before the market crashed ushering in the "Great Depression," Rosco began taking steps to put his vision into reality.

What was the dream? Simply to build the world's tallest skyscraper in New York City. People said it couldn't be done, the timing was not right, it was an impossible project, and more. Some told him that it would be a financial catastrophe.

But in order to begin the project, Rosco sold all his stock at the height of the stock market's bull market. Not only did he sell all of his stock…he also convinced others to join him and do the same in order to support this project. Just a matter of days after he and his supporters had cashed in all their stock holdings, the market crashed, plunging the United States into the Great Depression which brought poverty and loss to millions of people. The timing was amazing. Rosco and his co-investors had maximized their holdings to the fullest.

If he and his fellow dreamers had not had the courage to invest all in their dream, they would have lost everything. The financing for their dream would have disappeared. The rest is history! One year later, in 1930, they began building their dream, the "Empire State Building." AND…completed it during the Depression years to have it finished and in place for the greatest financial recovery in this world's history.

To "risk" is to: "take a chance, venture, speculate, gamble, put in peril, dare, and to face uncertainty."

There are times in living when you have all the facts, all the answers, all the projections…but they will all amount to nothing unless someone is willing to take a risk. There is a time when it comes down to taking that leap of faith!

SOMEBODY said that it couldn't be done,
But he with a chuckle replied,
That maybe it couldn't, but he would be one,
Who wouldn't say so till he tried.
So he buckled right in, with the trace of a grin on his face.
If he worried he hid it.
And he started to sing as he tackled the thing
That couldn't be done,
AND HE DID IT!

Jesus looked at them and said to them, *"With men this is impossible, but with God all things are possible."*
(Matthew 19:26)

23

Little Eyes Are Upon You

There are little eyes upon you and they're watching night and day.
There are little ears that quickly take in every word you say.
There are little hands all eager to do anything you do;
And a little boy who's dreaming of the day he'll be just like you.

You're the little fellow's idol, you're the wisest of the wise.
In his little mind about you no suspicions ever rise.
He believes in you devoutly, holds all you say and do;
He will say and do in your way when he's grown up like you.

There's a wide-eyed little fellow who believes you're always right,
And his eyes are always opened, and he watches day and night.
You are setting an example every day in all you do,
For a little boy who wants to grow up to be just like you.

(Author is unknown)

24

Pistol Pete

"PISTOL" **Pete Maravich** was one of the greatest basketball players ever to play the game. He was inducted into the "Basketball Hall of Fame" as a testimonial to his talent. Ironically, he died shortly after receiving this award. His death was premature and totally unexpected. Here are some of his thoughts on his induction:

"These memories of Dad's goals for me were so clear on May 5, 1987, as I sat on a platform in Springfield, Massachusetts, surrounded by the most revered of all basketball achievers. Ironically, I once had told Dad back in my college days that if I ever made the Hall of Fame, I would refuse the award and tell them they had given it to the wrong guy. 'Give the award to my dad,' I had told him I'd say, 'because there is no way in the world I deserve the honor before he does.'

"As I look back now I finally feel as though I understand my inheritance. Dad handed me something beautiful and precious, and I will always be indebted to him. He gave me his life full of instruction and encouragement. He gave me hope in hopeless situations and laughter in the face of grim circumstances. Dad gave me an example of discipline unequaled, dedication unmatched. He gave me the privilege of seeing an unwavering faith when the darkness of life and death surrounded him. But, more than anything, my father became a symbol of what love and compassion can do in anyone's life, and I am happy to accept that love as his heir to a dream."

There is another aspect of Pistol Pete's life which was not generally known by most of his fans. Pete shares some of his conversion experience after his life of rebellion which had been lived in confusion. Here's how he said it in his book,

Heir to a Dream: "One of the first things I realized after I had settled things with God was the difference it made to be dedicated to something other than myself. Everything I had done since childhood was for selfish reasons, such as bringing adoration to myself, finding acceptance among my peers, and gratifying my ego. This selfishness had led to emptiness and no conventional way out of my self-centered life. After my conversion, I turned full circle. All the fame and fortune I had accumulated looked extremely pale when compared to the abundance of Christ in me."

The fears I had once possessed were wiped away…instead, my life was now filled with the light and love of Christ.

("Pistol" Pete Maravich)

Yet indeed I also count all things loss for the excellence of the knowledge of Christ Jesus my Lord, for whom I have suffered the loss of all things, and count them as rubbish, that I may gain Christ. (Philippians 3:8)

Condensed Wisdom

THE PRESIDENT of a management consultant firm called for a staff meeting in order to give them a special commission. He said, "Our job is to ensure increased organizational and personal effectiveness for all of our clients. For many years, we've done just that. Now, I want you to compile the best of our wisdom and experience on work success so that we might be able to pass it down to future and present clients as well as through the ages."

The consultant team eagerly left the conference room excited about this task. They worked long and hard to record their insights. About twelve months later, the finished product was given to the president. It totaled 1,427 pages. The president looked in astonishment at this massive masterpiece. "I'm sure this is a very accurate accumulation of your knowledge and experience," began the president, "but who is going to sit down and read all of this? Take it with you, revise it and shorten it."

Again the team went back to work condensing their material. Then with another sense of accomplishment they delivered the revised version to their president. "How many pages?" he asked.

"Only 324."

"I still fear people will not read it. Condense it down further."

With resignation, yet with discipline, the team condensed their findings to fewer than a hundred pages…then ten pages and finally down to a single page. Then, they figured that they had come this far so why not take it down to a single statement that would reflect all their combined findings concerning work success.

When the President read this single sentence, a broad smile crossed his face

and he congratulated the team. "Now, you have truly captured the essence of our work and research findings. As soon as employees and employers everywhere learn this simple truth, work effectiveness and work success will be greatly improved!"

So what was the sentence? Simply this:

"There ain't no free lunch!"

...and, there ain't!

If you are called to be a street sweeper, sweep streets even as Michelangelo painted, or Beethoven composed music, or Shakespeare wrote poetry. Sweep streets so well that all the hosts of heaven and earth will pause to say, here lived a great street sweeper who did his job well.

(Martin Luther King, Jr.)

And whatever you do in word or deed, do all in the name of the Lord Jesus, giving thanks to God the Father through Him.
(Colossians 3:17)

Positioned For Success

HOW DO YOU get yourself into position to become a vital member of a world championship professional basketball team? The team is the Chicago Bulls, known for their repeated championships as long as Michael Jordan lead the team. Well the answer may be different than you think. And no, I am not talking about Jordan. The man we're interested in is Scottie Pippen.

Consider...as a 6'-2", 145-pound point guard playing on his high school basketball team, his future prospects for playing ball at the college level were very dim to say the least.

The state college at Monticello failed to come through with the opportunity for a scholarship and the possibility of playing for which Pippen had hoped. He finally ended up at the University of Central Arkansas, not exactly a large basketball power, as a work-study "manager." The coach was Donald Dyer and Pippen was not even on the squad. However, he was positioned to learn and prepare himself by working with the team and practicing on his own skill-building disciplines.

Later, at Central Arkansas, he got the break for which he had positioned himself. Pippen grew to 6'-8" and produced an average of 23 points per game, eventually earning him a full ride scholarship which opened the door to playing at the professional level.

Yes...his chances were pretty slim. But Scottie Pippen never quit practicing! Coach Dyer kept a close eye upon his development and his constant preparation meant being ready when the opportunity presented itself. Now you know the story behind the man and his story.

Bill Bradley, former Senator and Presidential candidate, scholar and basketball star reminds us that, "When you are not practicing, remember, someone somewhere IS practicing; and when you meet him, he WILL win."

You have to be in a position for success to happen.
Success doesn't go around looking for someone
to stumble upon it.

He who has a slack hand becomes poor, but the hand of
the diligent makes rich.
He who gathers in summer is a wise son;
He who sleeps in harvest is a son who causes shame.
(Proverbs 10:4-5)

WWJD

Most people assume "WWJD" stands for "What Would Jesus Do?" This has been popularized, slogan-ized, worn on bracelets, plastered on bumper stickers and shown on all kinds of tee-shirts.

But...let's consider that these initials might really stand for "What Would Jesus Drive?"

One theory is that Jesus would tool around in an old Plymouth because the Bible says that "God drove Adam and Eve out of the Garden of Eden in a Fury." Or that later He will appear driving a White truck, as John the Revelator writes, "And I looked, and behold a White..."

But in Psalm 83, the Almighty clearly owns a Pontiac and a Geo. This passage urges the Lord to "pursue your enemies with your Tempest and terrify them with your Storm."

Then...perhaps God favors Dodge pickups because Moses' followers are warned not to go up a mountain "until the Ram's horn sounds a long blast."

However, there is some speculation that Moses also drove an Acura for a long time because there's a verse in Deuteronomy that states, "Moses was one hundred and twenty years old when he died. His eyes were not dim nor his Vigor diminished." It also appears that he would have had no trouble passing his vision driver's exam.

Some scholars insist that Jesus could have driven a Honda at some time but didn't like to talk about it. As proof, they cite a verse in John's gospel where Christ tells the crowd, "For I did not speak of my own Accord..."

Meanwhile, it appears that Moses also could have ridden an old British motorcycle as evidenced by this passage declaring that "the roar of Moses' Triumph is heard in the hills."

Joshua must have learned something from his leader about British vehicles. But his Triumph sports car must have had a hole in the muffler: "Joshua's Triumph was heard throughout the land."

That isn't the last we hear of Triumphs...be they sports cars or motorcycles. Paul the Apostle writes: "Now thanks be to God who always leads us in (a) Triumph..."

And, finally, following their Master's lead, the Apostles car-pooled in a Honda: "The Apostles were in one Accord..."

Oh...well, enjoy. A little bit of humor may brighten your day or somebody else's as you pass this along.

Just don't build a doctrine or practice along these verses grossly taken out of context. Just goes to show you that the Bible can be made to say just about anything. We have been admonished to study it carefully and thoughtfully because it's to be our guide for living and fathering.

Though a humorist may bomb occasionally, it is still better to exchange humorists than bombs. And...you can't fight when you're laughing.

(Jim Boren)

**Be diligent to present yourself approved to God,
A worker who does not need to be ashamed,
Rightly dividing the word of truth.
(II Timothy 2:15)**

Commitment

THIS HAPPENED in Borneo during the confrontation between Malaysia and Indonesia. A group of Gurkhas from Nepal were asked if they would be willing to jump from transport planes into combat against the Indonesians if the need arose. The Gurkhas had the right to refuse because they had never been trained as paratroopers.

While the Gurkhas usually agreed to anything, this time they rejected the plan. But the next day, one of their non-commissioned officers sought out the British officer who had made the request and said they had discussed the matter further and would jump...but only under certain conditions.

The British officer asked what those circumstances were.

The Gurkhan officer told him they would jump if the land where they were to jump was marshy or reasonably soft with no rocky outcrops because they were inexperienced in falling. The British officer considered this and said the dropping area would probably be over the jungle and there would be no rocky outcrops. That seemed all right so he asked if there was anything else.

"Yes," said the Gurkhan officer. The Gurkhas wanted the plane to fly as slowly as possible and no more than 100 feet high.

The British officer pointed out that the planes always flew as slowly as possible when dropping troops...but to jump from 100 feet was impossible. The Gurkhan wanted to know why?

The British officer explained that the parachutes wouldn't have time to open at that low a height. The Gurkhan leader was a bit surprised and said, "Oh, that's all right then. You didn't mention parachutes before. We'll jump with parachutes anywhere."

Wow! A story like that almost takes our breath away. Gurkhas willing to jump from an airplane without parachutes! How many of our institutions today could use such Gurkhan-like commitment and courage?

How about you, Dad? Do you have that kind of commitment to being a father in spite of life's circumstances? What kind of courage will you display in the face of adversity? Courage and commitment can free us from the flimsy excuses and enclosures that fear might have built around us! Go for it! Do it! Make a fresh commitment!

There's a difference between interest and commitment. When you're interested in doing something, you do it only when it's convenient. When you're committed to something, you accept no excuses; only results.

(Kenneth Blanchard)

Be strong and of good courage,
Do not fear nor be afraid of them;
For the Lord your God,
He is the One who goes with you.
He will not leave you nor forsake you.
(Deuteronomy 31:6)

Selflessness

JUST ABOUT EVERY SCHOOL STUDENT knows of Isaac Newton's famed encounter with a falling apple. Newton discovered and introduced the "laws of gravity" in the 1600s, which revolutionized astronomical studies.

But very few know that if it had not been for Edmund Halley, the world might never have learned from Newton.

It was Halley who challenged Newton to think through his original notions. Halley corrected Newton's mathematical errors and prepared geometrical figures to support his discoveries. Halley coaxed the hesitant Newton to write his great work, "Mathematical Principles of Natural Philosophy." Halley edited and supervised the publication and actually financed its printing even though Newton was wealthier and easily could have afforded the printing costs.

Historians call it one of the most selfless examples in the annals of science. Newton began almost immediately to reap the rewards of prominence while Halley received little credit.

He did use the principles to predict the orbit and return of the comet that would later bear his name, but only after his death did he receive any real acclaim. And because the comet only returns every seventy-six years, the notice is rather infrequent. Halley remained a devoted scientist who didn't care who received the credit as long as the cause was being advanced further.

Others in history have played Halley's role. John the Baptist said of Jesus Christ, "He must become greater; I must become less." Barnabas was content simply to introduce others to the greatness of Christ. Many anonymous, unheralded behind-the-scenes people have prayed for others to experience success. Such selflessness advances industry, advances the cause of Christ and furthers the purpose of the family.

A life without people, without the same people day after day, people who belong to us, people who will be there for us, people who need us and whom we need in return, may be very rich in other things, but in human terms, it is no life at all.

(Harold Kushner)

Two are better than one,
Because they have a good reward for their labor.
For if they fall, one will lift up his companion,
But woe to him who is alone when he falls,
For he has no one to help him up.
(Ecclesiastes 4:9-10)

A Father's ABCs

A ...lways trust your children to God's care.
B ...ring them to church.
C ...hallenge them to high goals.
D ...elight in their achievements.
E ...xalt the Lord in their presence.
F ...rown on evil.
G ...ive them love.
H ...ear their problems.
I ...gnore not their childish fears.
J ...oyfully accept their apologies.
K ...eep their confidences.
L ...ive a good example before them.
M ...ake them your best friends.
N ...ever ignore their endless questions.
O ...pen your heart to their love.
P ...ray for them by name.
Q ...uicken your interest in their spiritual development.
R ...emember their needs.
S ...how them the way of salvation.
T ...each them to work and how to work.
U ...nderstand they are still young.
V ...erify your statements.
W ...ean them from bad company.
eX ...pect them to obey.
Y ...earn for God's best for them.
Z ...ealously guide them in Biblical truth.

Vision

When APPLE COMPUTER fell into difficult times a while ago, Apple's young chairman, Steven Jobs, flew from Silicon Valley in California to New York City. He had one purpose in mind. It was to convince Pepsico's John Sculley to move west and take charge of this struggling, beginning company.

As the two men overlooked the Manhattan skyline from Sculley's beautiful penthouse office, the Pepsi executive started to decline the job offer as extended by Jobs.

"Financially," Sculley said, "you'd have to give me a million-dollar salary, a million-dollar bonus, and a million-dollar severance."

Flabbergasted, Steven Jobs gulped and agreed...IF Sculley would move to California. But Sculley would commit only to being a consultant from New York City. It seemed as though it would not work out at all.

At that, Jobs issued a challenge to Sculley: "Do you want to spend the rest of your life selling sugared water or do you want to change this world?"

Later, in his biography, *Odyssey,* Sculley admits Jobs's challenge "knocked the wind out of me." He went on to say that he'd become so caught up with his future at Pepsi, his pension and whether his family could adapt to life in California that an opportunity to "change the world" nearly passed him by. Instead, he put his life into perspective and went to Apple Computers and moved his family to California and the rest is history!

Now, sir, how many times have you turned down the opportunity to change this world?

And how is this world going to be changed? Simply one person at a time! One family at a time! One father at a time! A large part of the Christian message is letting people know what difference the gospel makes in a life. It's a life-changing life-style!

*We live in a time of paradox, contradiction, opportunity
and above all, change. To the fearful, change is threat-
ening because they worry that things may get worse. To
the hopeful, change is encouraging because they feel
things may get better. To those who have confidence in
themselves, change is a stimulus because they believe
one person can make a difference and influence what
goes on around them. These people are the
doers and the motivators.*

(Buck Rogers)

Behold, I tell you a mystery:
We shall not all sleep, But we shall all be changed...
In a moment,
In the twinkling of an eye, At the last trumpet!
(I Corinthians 15:51-52a)

Heroes are Hard to Find

WHO'S YOUR HERO? Who's your child's hero? If you are listening to journalists, talk show hosts or sportscasters, you'd have thousands of candidates or would you? But the odds are that you have to pause and think. These odds are that unless you have a hero among your family or friends you will draw a blank. In a recent Harris Interactive poll (8/20/01 for U.S. News) more than half could name no public figure alive today, no politician, no athlete, no scantily dressed diva that they considered heroic. One in six had no hero at all.

So what is a hero? It's a noun: 1. They go beyond the call of duty. 2. They act wisely under pressure. 3. They risk their life, their fortune, or their reputation. 4. They champion a good cause. 5. They serve as a calling to our higher selves.

At 1:22 a.m. on December 5, 1999, Las Vegas police officer Dennis Devitte was off-duty with friends in a restaurant when three gunmen burst in, shooting into the crowd. Devitte, age 41, a 20-year veteran of the force, pulled a small handgun out of his pocket and ran toward the gunmen, drawing their fire. Devitte's gun was too small to be accurate at anything but near point-blank range. So he kept his finger off the trigger and continued forward even after one bullet shattered his free hand, two others slammed into his thigh and another hit his groin. When he got close enough to fire, he hit one gunman fatally and scared off the others before collapsing with eight bullet wounds. "Please tell my wife I love her," said Devitte, who mistakenly thought he was dying. "I did the best I could. I hope I didn't hit anybody else." Dennis Devitte is a hero by our definition.

Of all the different ways in which you could be a hero, none is more breathtaking than selflessly risking one's life for another.

So who in this poll was considered the number one hero by more people than any other? JESUS CHRIST! Yes, that's right! Jesus Christ! Martin Luther King Jr. was number

two and Colin Powell was number three.

But dad, there's real hope for you to be a real hero! Almost one third of Americans told the pollsters that their hero is a friend or relative…most often it is their father or mother! And these findings are consistent with previous polls.

So…DAD, be the hero to your kids that they know you to be!

The life that you seek you will never find…
Gaze on the child who holds your hand,
Let your wife enjoy your repeated embrace!
For such is the destiny of mortal men.

(Gilgamesh, about 2,800 B.C.)

Then David said to the Philistine, "*You come to me with a sword, with a spear, and with a javelin. But I come to you in the name of the LORD of hosts, the God of the armies of Israel, whom you have defied. This day the LORD will deliver you into my hand…*"
So it was, when the Philistine arose and came and drew near to meet David, that David hurried and ran toward the army to meet the Philistine. Then David put his hand in his bag and took out a stone; and he slung it and struck the Philistine in his forehead, so that the stone sank into his forehead, and he fell on his face to the earth.
So David prevailed over the Philistine with a sling and a stone!
(I Samuel 17:45-46a, 48-50a)

What's Your Dream

DAVID McCLELLAND, the Harvard psychologist, has studied high achievers. He has concluded that successful people possess one common characteristic: "They dream incessantly about how to achieve their goals." Let's take that another step further. James Allen says, "Dreams are the seedlings of reality."

Here are some people who believed in themselves and their dream:

*After his older brother was shot down and killed in World War II, **Dick Clark** listened to the radio to ease his loneliness. He began dreaming of someday becoming an announcer on his own show. "American Bandstand" was the product of this man's dream.

*Ski instructor **Pete Seibert** was considered a bit crazy when he told of his dream to begin a ski resort. Standing on the summit of a mountain in the Gore Range in Colorado, Seibert finalized a dream he had since age twelve and began the challenge of convincing others that it was possible. Seibert's dream is now a reality called Vail.

*Two brothers-in-law had a dream of earning $75 a week. They started their own business that advertised a single product served thirty-one different ways. Their names were **Robbins** and **Baskins**. Today Baskin-Robbins Ice Cream is a dream come true for these founders…as well as ice-cream lovers everywhere.

*The Bank of America exists today because **A. G. Giannini** dreamed of starting a financial institution that served the "little guy." Although he was a high school drop out, Giannini believed his concept could become a national bank by making unheard of car and appliance loans. His dream was a reality by the time of his death.

*Living in a government-funded housing project in Pennsylvania, **Mike Ditka**

dreamed of escaping the mines of his home state. Capitalizing on his dream and athletic ability, he achieved notoriety as a pro football player and coach and now broadcaster.

These men and many more are a testimony to the exciting phenomenon that if you have a dream and nurture it, become passionate about it, and act upon it, you, too, can experience the realization of it! Help your children and family dream big dreams, too!

Dream lofty dreams, and as you dream, so shall you become. Your vision is the promise of what you shall one day be. One who cherishes a beautiful vision, a lofty ideal, will one day realize it!

(James Allen)

Now Joseph had a dream and he told it to his brothers...

Then he dreamed still another dream and told it to his brothers, and said, "*Look, I have dreamed another dream. And this time, the sun, the moon, and the eleven stars bowed down...*"
(Genesis 37:5, 9)

Persuasion

A VERY WEALTHY TEXAN was proud of his ranch, his holdings, his money and most of all, proud of his beautiful daughter. He planned a very special "coming out" party for her. He invited many of his closest associates and some of the most eligible bachelors in the area. After touring some of the 100,000 acres of mountains, rivers, grasslands and oil wells, he took everybody to the house. This was a very spectacular home and out back was the largest, fanciest swimming pool anybody had ever seen. There was also a special built-in barbecue at poolside.

The proud Texan then announced, "I have invited you all here today for a special reason. Please notice the swimming pool...it's stocked with alligators and piranhas. One of the things I value most is courage. Courage is what made me a billionaire! In fact, I value courage so much that if anybody is courageous enough to jump into that pool, swim through the alligators and piranhas to the other side...I'll give that man his choice: the hand of my beautiful daughter in marriage, 10,000 acres of the choicest ranch land, my house or a million dollars!"

Of course, everyone laughed nervously at the absurdity of the challenge! The rancher waited a while for his talk to sink in, then, seeing no takers, invited all of them to join him at the barbecue for steaks.

They all heard it at the same time...a loud SPLASH!

As one they turned in the direction of the pool to see a young man swimming for his life, across the pool, thrashing at the water, dodging the alligators, throwing himself over them, diving under water with the sounds of snapping following him. After several death-defying seconds, the man made it unharmed to the other side and lay panting on the apron of the pool.

The wealthy rancher ran in amazement to the swimmer, picked him up and

said, "Congratulations! You are indeed a man of courage and I intend to follow through on my promise. What will it be? My daughter's hand in marriage? Ten thousand acres of ranch land? My house? Or the one million dollars? Just tell me and it's yours!"

The swimmer, still breathing heavily, wiping the water from his face, finally caught his breath, looked at the host and said, "The only thing I want is the name of the man who pushed me into that pool!"

Okay, okay...so how many times have we needed a push? Just a nudge, a bit of persuasion to do what we should be doing?

I am tired of hearing about men with the "courage of their convictions." Nero and Caligula and Attila and Hitler had the courage of their convictions... But not one of them had the courage to examine their convictions or to change them, which is the true test of character.

(Sydney Harris)

Be strong and of good courage; do not be afraid nor be dismayed, for the Lord your God is with you wherever you go!
(Joshua 1:9b)

Holding On

ON A COMMUTER FLIGHT from Portland, Maine to Boston, Henry Dempsey, the pilot, heard an unusual noise near the rear of the small aircraft. He turned the controls over to his co-pilot and went back to check it out.

As he reached the tail section, the plane hit an air pocket, and Dempsey was tossed against the rear door. He quickly discovered the source of the mysterious noise. The rear door had not been properly latched prior to takeoff...and it flew open! He was instantly sucked out of the commuter jet!

The co-pilot, seeing the red light that indicated an open door, radioed the nearest airport, requesting permission to make an emergency landing. He reported that the pilot had fallen out of the plane and requested a helicopter search of that area of the ocean.

After the plane landed, they found Henry Dempsey...holding onto the outdoor ladder of the aircraft. Somehow he had caught the ladder, held on for ten minutes as the plane flew more than 200 mph at an altitude of 4,000 feet...and then at landing, kept his head from hitting the runway, which was a mere twelve inches away! It took airport personnel several minutes to pry Dempsey's fingers from the ladder!

I would think so. The news source of this story didn't give us a clue as to the mental condition of Dempsey following this incident. I wonder how well he slept at nights or how soon he was able to fly again. Interesting.

You, know, Dad, things in life may be turbulent at this time and you may not feel like holding on a bit longer. BUT...have you considered what the alternative will be like?

Many men fail because they quit too soon.
They lose faith when the signs are against them.
They do not have the courage to hold on, to keep fighting
in spite of that which seems insurmountable. If more of
us would strike out and attempt the "impossible," we very
soon would find the truth of that old saying that nothing
is impossible...abolish fear and you can
accomplish anything you wish.

(Dr. C. E. Welch, founder of Welch's Grape Juice)

**Jesus looked at them and said, "With men this is impossible,
but with God all things are possible."
(Matthew 19:26)**

The Cost of Raising a Child

WE HAVE OFTEN seen the breakdown of the cost of raising a child in today's world...but have you considered the rewards of raising a child?

The government recently calculated the cost of raising a child from birth to age 18 and came up with $160,140!! And that doesn't even take into account college tuition! For the fathers with kids, that figure can lead to all kinds of wild fantasies about all the money we could have invested if not for _____ (insert your child's name or names here). For others, that number might confirm the decision to remain childless.

But $160,140 isn't so bad if you break it down. It translates into $8,896.66 per year; $741.38 a month; $171.08 per week or a mere $24.44 a day! Just over a dollar an hour!

Still...you might think the best financial advice says don't have kids if you want to be rich. It's just the opposite. **Okay...so what do you get for your $160,140?**

Naming rights! First, middle and last for starters! Glimpses of God every day. Giggles under the covers every night. More love than your heart can hold. Butterfly kisses and Velcro hugs. Endless wonders over rocks, ants, frogs, worms, clouds and warm cookies. A hand to hold, usually covered with jam. A partner for blowing bubbles, flying kites, building sandcastles and skipping down the sidewalk in pouring rain. Someone to laugh yourself silly with no matter what the boss said or how your stocks performed that day.

For $160,140, you never have to grow up! You get to finger-paint, carve pumpkins, play hide-and-seek, catch lightning bugs and watch cloud formations. You have an excuse to keep reading the "Adventures of Piglet and Pooh," watching

Saturday morning cartoons, going to Disney movies and wishing on stars. You get to frame rainbows, hearts and flowers under refrigerator magnets.

For $160,140, there is no greater bang for your buck! You get to be a hero for retrieving a Frisbee off the garage roof, taking the training wheels off the bike, removing a splinter, filling the wading pool, coaxing a wad of gum out of bangs and coaching a baseball team that never wins but always gets treated to ice cream. You get a front row seat to history to witness the first step, first word, first bra, first date and first time behind the wheel!

For $160,140, you get to be immortal! You get another branch added to your family tree and if you're fortunate, a long list of limbs in your obituary called grandchildren and great-grandchildren. You get an education in psychology, nursing, criminal justice, communications, marketing, family relationships and human sexuality that no college can match.

In the eyes of your child, you rank right up there, next to God! You have all the power to heal a boo-boo, scare away the monsters under the bed, patch a broken heart, hold them close in a thunder storm, comfort them when others reject them, police a slumber party, ground them forever if needed.

Most importantly you get to love them without limits so that one day, just like you, they can love without counting the cost!

All of that and more for a mere $160,140 investment!

Missing the Circus

ONCE WHEN I WAS A TEENAGER, my father and I were standing in line to buy tickets for the circus. Finally, there was only one family between us and the ticket counter. This family made a big impression on me, a young teen. There were eight children, all probably under the age of twelve. You could tell they didn't have a lot of money. Their clothes were not expensive but they were clean. The children were well-behaved, all of them standing in line, two-by-two behind their parents, holding hands. They were excitedly jabbering about the clowns, elephants and other acts they would see that night. One could sense they had never been to the circus before. It promised to be a highlight in their young lives.

The father and mother were at the head of the pack standing proud as could be. The mother was holding her husband's hand, looking up at him as if to say, "You're my knight in shining armor." He was smiling and basking in pride. The ticket lady asked how many tickets he wanted. He proudly responded, "Please let me buy eight children's tickets and two adult's tickets so I can take my family." The lady quoted the price. The man's wife let go of his hand, her mouth dropped and the man's lip began to quiver.

The father leaned a little closer and asked, "How much did you say?" She repeated the price. He didn't have enough money. How was he supposed to tell his eight kids he didn't have enough money?

Seeing what was going on, my dad put his hand into his pocket, pulled out a $20 bill and dropped it on the ground. (We were not wealthy in any sense of the word!) My father reached down, picked up the bill, tapped the man on the shoulder and said, "Excuse me, sir, this fell out of your pocket."

The man knew what was going on. He wasn't asking for a handout but certainly appreciated the help in a desperate, heartbreaking, embarrassing situation. He looked straight into my dad's eyes, took my dad's hand in both of his, squeezed tightly onto the $20 bill and with his lip quivering and a tear streaming down his cheek, he replied, "Thank you, thank you, sir. This really means a lot to me and my family."

My father and I went back to our car and drove home. We didn't go to the circus that night but we didn't go without.

(Jim Petty of Lockport, Illinois)

Life itself can't give you joy or love,
Unless you really will it;
Life just gives you time and space,
It's up to you to fill it!
(Author is unknown)

Then Peter said, "Silver and gold I do not have,
but what I do have I give you."
(Acts 3:6b)

Possessions and Treasures

You possess a job…you treasure your
family.

You possess a house…you treasure your
home.

You possess a bank account…you treasure
your friends.

You possess a car…you treasure your
freedom.

You possess a great wardrobe…you treasure
your health.

You possess an appointment book…you
treasure your time.

You possess a heart…you treasure
love.

You possess a net worth…you treasure the
opportunity it gives you to serve.

(Leonard Sweet)

Murphy's Laws of Fatherhood

BY NOW, MOST FATHERS know all about "Murphy's Law": "If something can go wrong, it will."

Since Murphy first discovered and applied this law, there have been many revisions and updates. For example: It's been re-written as "Murphy's Flaw"...if anything can't go wrong it will. Or Fetridge has come on the scene with his version: "Important things that are supposed to happen do not happen, especially when people are looking."

"Fetridge's Law" was named by and for Claude Fetridge, an engineer working for NBC radio, who in 1936 came up with the idea of doing a live broadcast to report on the departure of the swallows from their roost at Mission San Juan Capistrano on St. John's Day, October 23rd. Fetridge's equipment-laden crew arrived to find that the swallows had left a day early. This law was all but forgotten until H. Allen Smith wrote of it in 1963 in an attempt to explain why a toothache that strikes suddenly on Sunday on the golf course disappears while walking up the stairs to the dentist's office on Monday.

Oh, well...you're catching on, but I have digressed. Herewith in the spirit of Murphy are the ten laws of fatherhood in living color. These are offered in the spirit of being helpful as additions to the original "Murphy's Law" and are not meant to depress you as a father. Hopefully there will be some encouragement to you who have thought these things happened only to you. So here goes...

TEN LAWS OF FATHERHOOD

I) If your baby manages to sleep for eight consecutive hours, none of those hours will happen to fall between 11:00 pm and 7:00 am.

II) The number of times your child will ask "why" is directly in proportion to the length of the book you happen to be reading to him/her at the time. If it's one of those little stubby books with only a word or two on a page, she/he won't ask any questions. But if you're in a hurry and she/he has asked for a particular Dr. Seuss book, not a single page will go by without a question.

III) The day your brand new off-white carpet has been installed your child will introduce you to "projectile" vomiting. Unless, of course, it's "stainmaster" carpet, in which case the child will

manage to hit the sofa and recliner, whichever one has not been treated with "Scotch-Guard". But in the case of both being treated, the child will spew it into an open drawer.

IV) When you have finally worked up the courage to have your new pastor and spouse over for a formal sit-down candlelight dinner, your child will utter their very first word. The good news is that the enunciation will be perfect…the bad news is that it will be the worst word you can imagine.

V) Just when you have recovered enough to convince the pastor that your child couldn't possibly have known what he/she was saying, the toddler will speak forth the second word. It's spoken as clearly as the first word…but you realize that the first spoken word was not actually the worst one you could have imagined.

VI) When you are brave enough to dress your child in real underwear instead of a diaper, this child will immediately refuse to tell you when it's time to go potty even though this child has been warning you each time, while in diapers. The exception is when you're in a football stadium crammed with 65,000 fans with two minutes left to play, your team is trailing by four points on the move and a time-out has been called. That's when your child utters those precious words: "Daddy…DADDY…I have to go potty!"

VII) To compound this problem-dilemma, you had read an article telling you that if you ignore your child at this juncture they will get some kind of complex which leads to bed-wetting until college days. It's first and goal from the nine yard line, now with 54 seconds left, the quarterback throws three passes which are dropped in the end zone, until you arrive at an empty men's room and while going through the motions, you miss the greatest catch ever made on fourth and nine in the end zone. It's history making.

VIII) The first time your child makes you proud as a father by answering the phone all by himself/herself…you find out that they hung up on somebody by the name of Ed McMahon who was calling about a magazine sweepstakes winner.

IX) If you are on a diet, your child will not touch the food they had insisted on putting on their plate at an expensive buffet-style restaurant where there are all kinds of signs posted about not taking more than you can eat and you feel guilty and obligated about it going to waste, so you eat it.

X) The next time you go to a restaurant (while still on the above diet), and intentionally order light, anticipating the opportunity to clean your child's plate, she/he will finish every bite every time.

Handwriting On the Wall

A VERY WEARY FATHER returned from the hardware store,
lugging some home repair supplies through the kitchen door.
Awaiting his arrival was his eight-year-old son,
anxious to relate what his younger brother had done.

"While I was out playing and Mom was on the phone,
T. J. took his crayons and wrote on the wall!
And it's on the new paper you just hung in the den.
I told him you'd be mad at having to do it all over again."

He let out a groan and furrowed his brow,
"Where is your little brother right now?"
He emptied his arms and with a purposeful stride,
marched to the closet where little brother had gone to hide.

He called his full name as he entered the room.
The little one trembled with fear...he knew that meant doom!
For the next ten minutes, dad ranted and raved
about the expensive wallpaper and how much he had saved.

Lamenting all the work it would take to repair,
he condemned his actions and total lack of care.
The more he scolded, the madder he got,
then stomped from the room, totally distraught!

He headed for the den to confirm his worst fears.
When he saw the wall, his eyes flooded with tears.
The message he read pierced his soul with a dart.
It said, "I love Mommy and Daddy," surrounded by a heart.

Well, the wallpaper remained, just as he found it,
With an empty picture frame hung to surround it.
A reminder to him, and indeed to all,
TAKE TIME TO READ THE HANDWRITING ON THE WALL!

*The longer you dwell on another's weakness, the more
you infect your own mind with unhappiness.*

(Hugh Prather)

**He who has knowledge spares his words,
And a man of understanding is of a calm spirit.
(Proverbs 17:27)**

The Young Farmer

THE YOUNG FARMER sat happily on the wagon seat as his spirited team trotted into town. He hitched the team to a hitching rack near a corner of the main business block and walked down the street to the general store to buy the week's groceries.

Hardly had he entered the store when some boys strolled past his team. With a flick of his wrist one of the thoughtless boys tossed a lighted firecracker under the wagon. At the burst of the firecracker, the team reared backward lunging against the lines that held them to the hitching post. The lines snapped like string and the frightened team, with ears laid back and manes flying, headed out of town at a full gallop.

At this moment, the young farmer stepped out of the store. Taking in this scene at a glance, he threw himself into the street just as the horses swept by. With a flying leap he reached for the nearest bridle and...miracle of miracles, he caught it. The running horses jerked his feet out from under him and dragged him along the side. But he held on as if his hands were welded to the bridle. In about 75 yards or so the team slowed and the farmer managed to get around in front of them. But the horses were not giving in so easily. The team heaved against the wagon tongue and reared on their hind legs with front hooves pawing at the air. Then down they came and a flying hoof struck the young farmer full in the face. Slowly the iron grip relaxed on the bridle and the figure slumped silently into the dust. Other men now reached the team and brought them under control.

They carried the dead man to the plank sidewalk and gently laid him down. Bitterly, one of the men spoke, "The fool! The crazy fool! Why didn't he let them go? They would have run themselves out on the prairie. He didn't have to die like

this. The crazy fool!"

It was then that they heard the sound from the wagon and every eye turned in that direction. Above the sideboards appeared the head, the blond head of a little boy crying for his daddy!

What's a dad to do? Especially when one of his own might be in danger? It's instinct to protect at any cost. Children can be so vulnerable, so susceptible to hurt, so naïve, so gullible, so needy. Where will help come from other than from a loving, caring father?

There is only one way to succeed in anything and that is to give everything. I do and I demand that my players do. Any man's finest hour is when he has worked his heart out in a good cause and lies exhausted on the field of battle…victorious!

(Vince Lombardi)

This is My commandment, that you love one another as I have loved you. Greater love has no one than this, than to lay down one's life…
(John 15:12-13a)

Forgiveness On the Golf Course

RELATIVELY UNKNOWN outside the golfing world, Ian Woosnam was playing in the prestigious British Open tournament (July, 2001). He had been on what one news service called a "downhill slide" in his career. But here he was atop the leader board, tied on the last day of the tournament, with four other golfers including eventual winner David Duvall. This may well have been Woosnam's last opportunity at winning another major golfing championship. Here's the story:

Ian Woosnam was pumped as he stood on the second tee Sunday. After nearly making a hole-in-one, he was leading in the final round of the British Open.

Bending over to tee up his ball, he straightened to his full 5-foot-4-height and turned to caddie Miles Byrne for a club. Instead, he got the shock of his golfing life.

"You're going to go ballistic," Bryne told him.

"Why?" asked Woosnam.

"We've got two drivers in the bag," the caddie replied.

Woosnam knew immediately what it meant. He had 13 other clubs in the bag. With two drivers, that made 15. Only 14 are allowed. The two stroke penalty he had to call on himself would knock him out of the lead. "At that moment, I felt like I had been kicked in the teeth," Woosnam said.

When the day was over, Woosnam did fall four strokes short of the winner and was left to wonder what might have been had one of the worst gaffs in a major golfing championship history not happened.

But the response here is what captures my attention. First, Byrne said, "You want me to stand here and make excuses? There is no excuse. The buck stops at me. My fault, two-shot penalty, end of story."

Then secondly, there was Woosnam's response: "It's the biggest mistake he will make in his life. He won't do it again. He's a good caddie. He will have a severe talking to when I get in, but I'm not going to sack him."

The crowd sympathized with Woosnam and rose to their feet and gave him a standing ovation as he and Bryne approached the 18th green.

Failure. Responsibility. Honesty. Understanding. Mercy. Forgiveness. I think I've read this story on the pages of the Bible before.

Since nothing we intend is ever faultless, and nothing we attempt ever without error, and nothing we achieve without some measure of finitude and fallibility we call humanness, we are saved by forgiveness.

(David Augsburger)

And forgive us our debts,
As we forgive our debtors.
For if you forgive men their trespasses, your Heavenly Father
will also forgive you.
But if you do not forgive men their trespasses, neither will your
Father forgive your trespasses.
(Matthew 6:12, 14-15)

A Thought On Marriage

WITH THIS WORLD SPINNING so fast and relationships being so few, a marriage may be the only stable and secure commitment a couple will know throughout their hurried life. It must be placed on a higher priority.

John Fischer, a Christian musician, offers some sound advice along these lines. It seems that John had rented a room from an elderly couple who had been married longer than most people live. But even though time had wrinkled their hands, stooped their postures and slowed them down, it hadn't diminished the excitement and love they had toward each other. Intrigued, the singer finally had an opportunity to ask the old man the secret of his success as a husband. "Oh," said the old gentleman with a twinkle in his eye, "that's simple. Just bring her roses on Wednesday...she never expects them then."

That short conversation inspired a song:

> *Give her roses on Wednesday,*
> > *when everything is blue,*
> *Roses are red and your love must be new.*
> *Give her roses on Wednesday,*
> > *keep it shining through*
> *Love her when love's the hardest thing to do.*
>
> *Love isn't something you wait for,*
> *Like some feeling creeping up from behind.*
> *Love's a decision to give more.*
> *And keep giving all of the time.*

Give her roses on Wednesday…

It's easy to love when it's easy,
When you're in a Friday frame of mind.
But loving when living gets busy,
Is what love was waiting for all the time.

Give her roses on Wednesday…
(Song by John Fischer)

The kind of marriage you make depends upon the kind of person you are. If you are a happy, well-adjusted person, the chances are your marriage will be a happy one. If you have made adjustments so far with more satisfaction than distress, you are likely to make your marriage and family adjustments satisfactorily. If you are discontented and bitter about your lot in life, you will have to change before you can expect to live happily ever after.
(Evelyn Duvall and Reuben Hill)

Marriage is honorable among all, and the bed undefiled;
but fornicators and adulterers God will judge.
Let your conduct be without covetousness; be content with such things as you have.
For He Himself has said, "I will never leave you nor forsake you."
(Hebrews 13:4-5)

Integrity

PHIL DONAHUE tells of a time when he was starting out as a young television reporter and had been sent to cover a mine disaster:

It was late at night. Snow was on the ground. It was freezing cold. The rescue was down in the mine shaft. The worried relatives and friends were gathered at the opening of the mine, waiting anxiously for some word of hope.

Someone began to sing, *"What a friend we have in Jesus..."* Other people joined in the singing, *"All our sins and griefs to bear..."* Still more voices joined in, *"What a privilege to carry everything to God in prayer."*

Then it was quiet. A minister stepped out of the crowd and said, "Let us pray." It was a brief touching prayer. It was such a moving scene that Donahue said he got goose bumps.

The only problem was that it was so cold the television camera froze up and didn't catch the scene. Donahue held the camera against his body and rubbed it to get it functioning. He finally got it working and went to the minister and asked him to repeat that prayer.

The minister said, "No."

Donahue said, "I'm a TV reporter. I represent 260 stations. Millions of people will be able to see you and hear that beautiful prayer."

The minister said, "No."

Donahue then said, "Maybe you didn't understand. I'm not representing some local TV station. I'm with CBS. The whole nation will be able to see this."

The old country preacher said, "No," turned his back and walked away.

Donahue was dumbfounded and furious! He couldn't understand it. But about a year later he said that it hit him. He wrote that he realized he was witnessing

something called "integrity." He said, "The man wouldn't show biz for Jesus. He wouldn't sell his soul, not even for TV, not even, praise God, CBS!"

"Integrity" is defined in the *Random House College Dictionary* as: "adherence to moral and ethical principles; soundness of moral character; honesty." And it's in short supply in today's societies. Dad…it's true that you can't change the entire world, but, what about your parenting? You can make a difference! Integrity marks a real man!

A Chinese general put it this way: "If the world is to be brought to order, my nation must first be changed. If my nation is to be changed, my hometown must be made over. If my hometown is to be reordered, my family must first be set right. If my family is to be regenerated, I myself must first be."

(A. Purnell Bailey)

The refining pot is for silver and the furnace for gold,
And a man is valued by what others say of him.
(Proverbs 27:21)

Anticipation

HE WAS JUST A LITTLE GUY. His mother had died when he was only a toddler and his father, trying to be both mommy and daddy, was single parenting. His dad had planned a very special outing on the next day for the two of them. Among the plans for this big day was a picnic in the park. So there had been great excitement as the two had anticipated a special day on this Saturday. They finalized their plans and packed their picnic lunch and then it was time for bed so they could have an early start in the morning.

But this little fellow, as you might guess, couldn't sleep. He tossed and turned in excitement, thinking about tomorrow. Finally he jumped out of bed and ran into his father's bedroom, where his dad was about to drop off to sleep. As he shook him, his father's eyes opened.

"What are you doing up?" asked the father.

"I can't sleep," replied the excited boy.

"Why?"

"Daddy, I'm really excited about tomorrow!"

"Well, I'm sure you're excited but if you don't get back into bed and get some sleep, it won't be such a great day tomorrow," replied the father, "so now, why don't you run down the hall, get into bed and get some good sleep."

So he trudged off down the hall, got into bed and before long, sleep came…to the dad, that is. Presently, dad felt once more those tiny hands, pushing and shoving to awaken him. But before angry words could spill out of his mouth, he saw in the eyes of his son the absence of a mother…long gone…and the loneliness of a child too long without her. Then he felt those slender arms about his neck and he

heard the words, "Daddy, I just wanted to thank you for tomorrow!"

For children, anticipation is something very special. Hope and excitement are such an essential part of childhood. And this presents a challenge for fathers. Carefully plant hope and anticipation…which may be more exciting than the actual event. Delayed gratification is a life lesson that is learned through carefully laid plans and what an important life lesson this is. Teach it well.

Children may doubt what you say…
but they will believe what you do!

FATHERS, do not provoke your children,
lest they become discouraged.
And whatever you do, do it heartily, as to the Lord
and not to men.
(Colossians 3:21, 23)

Failure In Perspective

THE YOUNG ASPIRING PITCHER knew he was in trouble when the Little League coach came to the mound, asked for the ball and said, "Son, I think it's time I have someone come in to relieve you."

"But," the pitcher argued, "I struck this guy out the last time I pitched to him."

"I know," the coach said with empathy, "but this is the same inning."

Dentists' mistakes are pulled. Carpenters turn theirs into sawdust. Doctors' failures are buried. Lawyers' mistakes get put into prisons. Preachers leave their failures behind. Mechanics replace the engine. Politicians resign. HOWEVER, too often, like the young pitcher, most of our failures end up out in the open for all to see!

It can be embarrassing to have our mistakes, stumbles, blunders, wrong choices and failures out there in the open, exposed to everybody. But before the pity party begins...you can always remind yourself that it could have been much worse.

For example...how would you like to have listed on your resume this little item: "Designed the Tower of Pisa (which is leaning)?" Today, that tower is a bit more than twenty feet out of perpendicular. Now the guy that designed that building and planned the foundation to be only ten feet deep for a 179-foot-tall building on sandy soil happened to be a sandwich or two short of a full picnic that day.

None of us will ever know what we can achieve until we give it a try. If we make a mistake, come short of the goal, or totally mess up...so what's the big deal? That's why erasers were invented! Keep your failures in perspective. It's just another way not to do something. They are only temporary and only as big or disastrous as you will allow them to become.

Failure is a part of success! Chemist Paul Ehrlich discovered a drug to treat those patients with syphilis. It was named "Formula 606," because the first 605 tests were a failure!

Fear of failure brings fear of taking risks...and you're never going to get what you want out of life without taking some risks. Remember, everything worthwhile carries the risk of failure!

(Lee Iacocca)

To You, O Lord, I lift up my soul.
For You, Lord, are good,
and ready to forgive,
And abundant mercy to all those who call upon You!
(Psalm 86:4b-5)

Defeating Death

UGANDAN BISHOP FESTO KIVENGERE gives the following account of the execution of three men from his diocese by firing squad:

February 10 began as a sad day for us in Kabale. People were commanded to come to the stadium and witness the execution. A silent crowd of about 3,000 gathered to watch.

I had permission from the authorities to speak to the men before they died. They brought the men in a truck and unloaded them. They were handcuffed, and their feet were chained. The firing squad stood at attention. As I walked into the center of the stadium, I was wondering what to say. How do you give the gospel to doomed men who are probably seething with rage? I approached them from behind and as they turned to look at me, what a sight! Their faces were alight with an unmistakable glow and radiance. Before I could say anything, one of them burst out:

"Bishop, thank you for coming! I wanted to tell you. The day I was arrested, in my prison cell, I asked the Lord Jesus to come into my heart. He came in and forgave me all my sins! Heaven is now open and there is nothing between me and my God! Please tell my wife and children that I am going to be with Jesus. Ask them to accept Him into their lives as I did."

The other two men told similar stories, excitedly raising their hands which rattled their handcuffs.

I felt that what I needed to do was to talk to the soldiers, not to the condemned. So I translated what the men had said into a language the soldiers understood. The military men were standing there with guns cocked and bewilderment on their faces. They were so dumbfounded that they forgot to put the hoods over the men's faces!

The three faced the firing squad standing close together. They looked toward the people and began to wave, handcuffs and all. The people waved back. Then shots were fired and the three were with Jesus.

We stood in front of them, my heart throbbing with joy, mingled with tears. It was a day never to be forgotten. Though dead, the men spoke loudly to all of Kigezi District and beyond, so that there was an upsurge of life in Christ, which challenges death and defeats it!

The next Sunday, I was preaching to a huge crowd in the hometown of one of the executed men. Again, the feel of death was over the congregation. But when I gave them the testimony of their man, and how he died, there erupted a great song of praise to Jesus!

Many turned to the Lord there!

(Bishop Festo Kivengere)

They cast him out of the city and stoned him. And the witnesses laid down their clothes at the feet of a young man named Saul.
And they stoned Stephen as he was calling on God and saying, "Lord Jesus, receive my spirit."
Then he knelt down and cried out with a loud voice, "Lord, do not charge them with this sin."
And when he had said this, he fell asleep.
(Acts 7: 58-60)

Point of Light Jock

HAROLD REYNOLDS, pro baseball player, just assumed his status in the public eye would fade after he left baseball in 1995 after 12 seasons. He joined ESPN's Baseball Tonight as a studio analyst in 1996 and didn't think differently until the 1996 All-Star game in Philadelphia. This was his first major assignment away from the studio desk.

"I'm walking through the hotel and people are recognizing me, saying, 'Hey, I love the show'," Reynolds said. "Then I go to the stadium and it's like I'm the man. It was ridiculous. I couldn't believe the response. That was my first understanding of ESPN's platform…that we go into millions of homes every day."

Reynolds is a three-time Gold Glove-winning second baseman who led the American League in steals (60) in 1988. He is more famous now than he was in 10 years with the Mariners and one year playing for the Orioles and Angels.

"Strangely enough, major league baseball was my training ground," he says of dealing with a high profile. "My platform has broadened and changed an awful lot in the past six years."

Reynolds has used this expanded platform to talk about his love for Jesus Christ. It's through relationships and in speaking engagements where he shares his faith.

"I've always been an encourager," Reynolds said. "I was always taught that life and death are in the power of the tongue. A person can be a blessing or a curse, and I choose to be a blessing. People see me on TV and say I'm so positive…I'm not going to talk a lot of negative talk, because there are too many good things to say."

He is the first athlete to receive a commendation as one of the elder President Bush's "Thousand Points of Light."

(Thanks to Sports Spectrum, Sept./Oct. 2001)

In baseball, there was a verse (Jeremiah 29:11) I went to when I was scuffling, when I had an 0-fer. And that's the perspective most Christians have, to go there when they are having a tough time and be reminded that God has a plan. But that's not the message at all. The message of Christ is 'I've got a plan, let's rejoice'!

(Harold Reynolds)

For I know the thoughts that I think toward you, says the LORD, thoughts of peace and not of evil, to give you a future and a hope. (Jeremiah 29:11)

Laugh at the Game

TOO OFTEN, WE GUYS have a way of taking our athletic pursuits much too seriously. We've all heard those horror stories about parents who also take the sporting activities of their kids with too much intensity. Well, here's a very small collection of some "sporting HA-HAs" for your consideration:

*Ever play football with true "dumb jocks?" Haven't we all. They could pass as steroid children whose cholesterol counts were higher than their SAT scores. Richard, a big, strong, articulate lineman, appeared on television as a participant in the game show, *Wheel of Fortune*. He managed to get ahead by $300 when he interrupted by asking, "Pat, may I buy a vowel, please? Can you give me a K?"

*It happens at a Little League game. A nine-year-old rookie came up to bat against an all-star pitcher who was twelve. The pitcher threw his fast ball. "Strike one," the umpire called out.

The young batter said, "C'mon ump, that wasn't a strike!"

The ump asked, "Why? Did you see it?"

The rookie replied, "No! But it sounded high!"

*A high school football coach was asked by news reporters why his team had lost the game to the league champs. Not one of their running plays had gained any yardage in the game. Coach answered: "We were tipping off our running plays. They knew exactly where we were going to run. Every time we broke from the huddle, two of our running backs were laughing and the other one was as white as a sheet."

*Then there was the recruiter who was bringing the young player to the location of the university. He had never flown on a plane and had no idea about time changes. They were flying from Atlanta, Georgia to Knoxville, Tennessee. The counter clerk said, "The plane leaves at 4:00 pm and arrives in Knoxville at 3:45. Would you like two tickets?"

The astonished prospective recruit replied, "No! I don't want a ticket on that plane but I sure do want to see it take off!"

*Then...there's always golf. Todd is a wild golfer. He has to tee off before he knows what course he's playing. He turns it into a contact sport. One day he finally managed to hit a drive 250 yards straight. It was a great shot, except it hit a man on the head. The part that really ticked Todd off the most was when the man pulled off the highway and came running and found him!"

Oh, well! Enjoy your sports endeavors...but don't forget your sense of humor.

A sense of humor has been linked with longevity. It is a possibility that the mental attitude reflected in a lively sense of humor is an important factor predisposing some people toward long life.

(Raymond Moody)

This day is holy to the LORD your God; do not mourn nor weep. Then he said to them, "Go your way, eat the fat, drink the sweet, and send portions to those for whom nothing is prepared; for this day is holy to our LORD.
Do not sorrow,
FOR THE JOY OF THE LORD IS YOUR STRENGTH!
(Nehemiah 8:9b-10)

A Father's Ten Precepts

1. *HE makes himself responsible for his children's behavior.*

2. *HE is never blinded by love from recognizing and correcting his child's weakness.*

3. *HE makes his child feel secure.*

4. *HE shares in his child's activities.*

5. *HE has a child's complete confidence.*

6. *HE always is available to help solve youthful problems.*

7. *HE doesn't demand filial devotion...he wins it.*

8. *HE recognizes and accepts as largely his, the responsibility for his child's mental and spiritual development.*

9. *HE contributes to making the home the child's haven.*

10. *He strives to be honest with his children.*

(Author is unknown)

How to Become Player of the Year

ANEMIA is a condition in which your blood is deficient in red blood cells and volume. If this is not treated…you could die. If you live, you are weakened and fatigued.

This is the diagnosis given to a young boy in Worthing, Texas some years ago. The doctor also told him he would never be able to compete in sports…especially football. But that boy had a dream to play football and prove the doctor wrong.

He entered high school as a freshman and was told he was too small and too weak to play. So he became the team manager. He would stay after the team went home, he ran laps, he did wind sprints and lifted weights. His sophomore year he told his father his goal was to make the team…he was issued a uniform, but never played. He still stayed after practice, alone, to work out and run.

Then in his junior year, he told his dad he wanted to get into at least one game. The last game of the season his team was ahead and he played the entire fourth quarter. After that last game…he told his father he wanted to play in every game his senior year and earn a college scholarship. He got that chance to go to Baylor University. After injuries to three other linebackers in his first year he was moved from number four on the depth chart to starting linebacker. In his junior and senior years he was a unanimous choice for All-American. He signed a pro contract as a second-round draft pick of the Super Bowl Champion Chicago Bears.

Mike Singletary wound up being one of the best middle-linebackers to ever play in the National Football League. He anchored one of the best defenses in NFL history and was honored as "NFL Defensive Player of the Year" more than once.

IF he had listened to all the limitations others had placed on him… Mike would never have reached his goal!

Our lesson? Do what is inside of you. Reach for your goals, regardless of what others may tell you. Implant these concepts deep into the heart, mind and soul of your children, too!

It must be born in mind that the tragedy of life doesn't lie in not reaching your goal. The tragedy lies in having no goal to reach. It isn't a calamity to die with dreams unfulfilled, but it is a calamity to not dream. It is not a disgrace not to reach the stars, but it is a disgrace to have no stars to reach for. Not failure, but low aim is sin!

(Helmut Schmidt)

I do not count myself to have apprehended; but one thing do, forgetting those things which are behind and reaching forward to those things which are ahead, I press toward the goal for the prize of the upward call of God in Christ Jesus.
(Philippians 3:13-14)

Together We Can Make It

BOB BUTLER lost his legs in a 1965 land mine explosion in Vietnam. He returned home a war hero. Twenty years later, he proved once again that heroism comes from inside, from the heart. Here's the story:

Butler was working in his garage in a small town in Arizona. It was a hot summer day when he heard a woman's scream coming from the backyard of a nearby home. He quickly rolled his wheelchair toward the house but the shrubbery prevented him access. So he got out of his chair and crawled through the dirt and bushes. "I had to get there," he says. "It didn't matter how much it hurt."

When Butler managed to get to the edge of the swimming pool, three-year-old Stephanie Hanes was lying on the bottom. She had been born without arms and had accidentally fallen in the water and could not swim. Her mother was standing over her baby screaming frantically at the pool edge. Butler took in this scene quickly and immediately dove to the bottom of the pool and brought little Stephanie up to the pool deck. Her body was blue, she had no pulse and wasn't breathing.

He immediately went to work performing CPR to revive her while Stephanie's mother called 911. She was told that the paramedics were unavailable because they were already out on a call. She sobbed, grabbed Butler's shoulders and felt helpless.

As he continued with his CPR, he reassured her, "Don't worry. I was her arms to get out of the pool. It'll be okay. I am now her lungs. Together we can make it."

Some moments later, the little girl coughed, regained consciousness and began to cry. Mother hugged her little daughter close and rejoiced! Then she turned to Butler and asked him how he knew it would be okay.

"When my legs were blown off in the war, I was alone in a field," he told her. "No one was there to help except a little Vietnamese girl. As she struggled to drag me into her village, she whispered in broken English, 'It okay. You can live. I be your legs. Together we make it.'"

He told the mother that this was his chance to return the favor.

82

Courage is doing what you're afraid to do. There can be no courage unless you're scared."

(Eddie Rickenbacker)

Be strong and of good courage,
do not fear nor be afraid of them;
for the LORD your God,
He is the One who goes with you.
He will not leave you nor forsake you.
(Deuteronomy 31:6)

Perspective

THERE WAS A PARTICULAR CO-ED who had two problems common to many college students: grades were lower than expected and she was running out of money. She also knew that she was forced to communicate both of these problems to her mom and dad. There was another problem...she knew they would have some problems in understanding the reasons why. After giving her problems some considerable thought, she came up with a solution. She used a most creative approach in order to soften the blows of reality. So this is the e-mail she sent home:

Dear Mom and Dad:
Greetings! Just thought I'd drop you this e-mail to clue you in on my future plans. I've fallen madly in love with a guy named Pete. He quit high school after grade eleven to get married. It didn't work out so he got a divorce about a year later and he has one little boy.
We have been going steady for about two months and plan on getting married this spring. Until then, I have decided to move into his apartment so I can help him with the costs as he has no job. Also, I think I just might be pregnant.
At any rate, I dropped out of college last week.

That was in the first e-mail. The next e-mail went like this:

*MOM and DAD...I just want you to know that **EVERYTHING** I wrote in my last e-mail is false! NONE of it is true!*
But, Mom and Dad, it is true that I got a C- in French and I flunked algebra

and will have to take it over. It is true that I'm going to need some more
money for my next semester tuition payments.

Pretty sharp young lady! It's amazing but bad news can sound like good news if it is seen from a different perspective. So much of life depends on where you are. The secret of any life problem is tackling it from the correct perspective...especially when dealing with your kids.

Perspective is really self-discipline in action.

To everything there is a season,
A time for every purpose under heaven:
A time to be born,
And a time to die;
A time to plant,
And a time to pluck what is planted;
A time to weep,
And a time to laugh;
A time to mourn,
And a time to dance;
A time to keep silence,
And a time to speak...
(Ecclesiastes 3:1-2, 4, 7)

A Real Dad

September 11, 2001, is a date this is forever seared into the soul of Americans. It was the most horrifying act of terrorism as fuel laden jet liners rammed into the twin towers of the World Trade Center in New York City, crashed into the ground in Pennsylvania, and another crashed our Pentagon in Washington, D.C. Out of these tragedies have come hundreds of stories of bravery and wonderful people who lost their lives.

One who lost his life was 53-year-old Steven Morello Senior. When Steven Jr. had wanted to drop out of college to pursue his dream of starting a band, his dad gave him some very different advice. It was unexpected. He said, "You've got the rest of your life to go to college. When you want to go back, I'll support you and pay for it."

Some time later when Steven Jr. made the choice to stay at home and care for their new baby while his wife went back to work, his dad agreed with this choice and said, "Your family is your priority."

This is how he lived his life according to his children. He worked for the insurance company, Marsh and McLennan, with offices in the World Trade Center. Alfia, his daughter, was following in her father's footsteps for a career choice but failed in her first attempt at her stock-broker's examination. Then her father stayed up late with her three nights in a row to help her study for the next test. When she had answered the last question correctly, he took her face in his hands and gently said, "I've never loved you more than I do right now."

He was married for 33 years. During that time he only traveled once without his wife at his side to share this part of his life. Friday nights were family nights…he loved to be a couch-potato with his kids. Morello Jr. said: "Our world revolved around him. We sit on my parents' bed, eat pizza and watch TV."

And as a fitting final tribute to a father whose life was snuffed out in this tragedy, Steven said, "My father wasn't a symbol of destructive capitalism. He was a loving human being who took care of his family."

(Adapted, *U.S.NEWS & WORLD REPORT*, 9/24/2001)

NOW, WE CAN START TO LOOK ACROSS THE VALLEY FOR SIGNS OF HOPE.

(Thomas McDowell)

Yea, though I walk through the valley of the shadow of death,
I will fear no evil;
For You are with me;
Your rod and Your staff,
They comfort me.
You prepare a table before me in the presence of my enemies;
You anoint my head with oil;
My cup runs over.
Surely goodness and mercy shall follow me
All the days of my life;
And I will dwell in the house of the LORD
Forever.
(Psalm 23:4-6)

Fastballs and Faith

It was a muggy night in late October in Miami with Game 7 of the 1997 World Series on the line. This series was being played between the Cleveland Indians and the Florida Marlins. It was the deciding game…the score was knotted at two runs each in the bottom of the 11th inning. Craig Counsell hit a slow ground ball to Tony Fernandez at second base. He hurried to turn it into an inning ending double play but he missed it and turned to watch it roll slowly into the outfield! This set up the go-ahead run and a 3-2 Marlins World Series victory over his Indians!

This was not a typical Fernandez error. He had earned a World Series ring in 1993; appeared in four All-Star games; awarded four Gold Glove citations (1986-1989). He holds the major league record for career fielding percentage by a short-stop (.980); and the Toronto Blue Jays' all-time record for the most triples (70). BUT it was that error on the night of October 26, 1997 that caused the most attention as well as the best platform from which he can talk about his relationship with Jesus Christ.

He was born into a Baptist pastor's family…one of eleven children, in a tiny house behind a ballpark in San Pedro de Macoris in the Dominican Republic. He made the jump to professional baseball at only 17 years of age. He spent six days a week at the ball park but each Sunday, attending church was a must. Tony says, "It was go to church or get a spanking."

By 1983 he was a major league shortstop. He arrived for spring training in 1984, married, but with a cast on his left hand. He began to feel something was missing, something that baseball or a new marriage could not fill. Jesse Barfield and Roy Lee Jackson played on the team and were sharing their faith with Tony. One day after a baseball chapel service, Fernandez decided it was time to give his

life to Jesus Christ. "I remember walking out of the chapel, across the locker room, and I called to Jesse. I said, 'Jesse, hey, I think I'm ready to accept Christ.' He said, 'Do you think you're really ready?' Then he looked me straight in the eyes and said, 'I think you are,' and he called Roy Lee Jackson and the other ones (from the chapel service). I remember that right at that moment I gave my life to Jesus."

Fernandez admits that dealing with *that* error and loss wasn't easy, "It was particularly hard on my five children. One son was crying to me after the game, and I told him to remember it's just a game. If you do your best, that's all you can do. If the outcome is different than what you expected, you can't change that. You have to always be ready to accept the good and the bad."

If your life is based on earthly success, then when you have disaster you're in trouble. That is why I was able to handle it very, very effectively. I think God gave me this platform to glorify Him. My main purpose on this earth is to serve Him no matter what, and be obedient to His calling.

(Tony Fernandez)

**In all your ways acknowledge Him,
And He shall direct your paths.
(Proverbs 3:6)**

It's All About a Mouse

This is about a mouse and a man! The man saw a golden opportunity run across his foot. I'm sure he didn't see all that much of an opportunity at that moment. Let's go back in time to a garage located in the Midwest.

Seated in this garage was a struggling, half-starving illustrator who was attempting to make a living with his drawings. He was discouraged. He couldn't seem to get a break. As he sat there at his drawing pad searching for some kind of an idea…a mouse ran across his foot. And he watched that mouse run around the garage not seemingly afraid of the illustrator.

I don't know about you…but mice are not welcome in my house. They make a nuisance of themselves, they chew on things, they eat things, they make a mess, they scare wives and kids and smell up the place. This young illustrator watched the mouse scurry about and then into the hole from which he'd appeared. He was thinking about how miserable his chances were of succeeding as an artist. It was a pretty bleak outlook. THEN…he began to imagine things about that pesky, persistent mouse and he began to doodle and draw.

America and the rest of the world have been changed by a man and a mouse. A mouse which ran across a foot. He drew the mouse and named it Mickey and created a mate named Minnie. Yes, you've guessed right, the man's name was Walt Disney and now you know the rest of this simple little story.

The next time you see a sign of failure, maybe in the form of a mouse, give it a second look. It might be the thing which gets your attention and turns your world around. Walt Disney built an empire on nothing more than a silly little mouse! He looked down…then looked up! He noticed something little and then soared to great heights! Don't overlook the insignificant.

Well, some people create their own opportunities; others go where opportunities are the greatest; others fail to recognize opportunity when they are face to face with it.
(Walter P. Chrysler)

I am as strong this day as on the day that Moses sent me;
just as my strength was then, so now is my strength for war, both for
going out and for coming in.
Now therefore, give me this mountain!
(Joshua 14:11-12a)

Returns On an Investment

WHEN ORVIL REID went to Mexico as a missionary he met twelve-year-old Jose Gonzalez. Jose had come to Guadalajara to find work. He slept in the ovens of a bakery after they had cooled at night.

Reid invited Jose to live in the student home he had started. The boy worked in a print shop while going to school. He eventually graduated from medical school at the University of Guadalajara and became a leading internist and cardiologist. For a while Dr. Gonzalez was chief resident at Methodist Hospital in Dallas before returning to Guadalajara where he is now Director of the Mexican-American Hospital.

Orvil Reid is retired and living in Dallas. Some time ago he suffered a stroke. When Reid's wife called a doctor friend, to her surprise, Dr. Gonzalez, who happened to be visiting in Dallas, answered the phone. Together, the two doctors rushed the retired missionary to the hospital. Reid suffered partial paralysis but is recovering. Reid had once extended a hand to Jose who was in need. The life he once touched has become the helping hand which helped save his life!

Here's another story of investing:

Julius Hickerson was a promising young doctor who could have made a fortune in the United States but chose to go to Columbia as a missionary. He had been there for two years with little visible results. Then he was tragically killed in a plane crash as he attempted to take medical supplies to a remote village. In that wreckage, some of the natives found a Bible written in their own language, all marked up, which they began to read. Soon people became Christians. They began a church and soon went to other villages to preach the gospel of Jesus Christ.

Some time later, unaware of what had taken place, the Southern Baptists sent a missionary back into that area. He was surprised to find this mission field already

evangelized! He asked how this had happened without a missionary and one of the natives showed him a Bible...and on the inside of the cover was the name: *"Julius Hickerson!"*

Investment in others, particularly your children, or the investment of yourself in others always brings lasting results! However, these results may not be immediately realized. In fact we may never know the returns until this life is over.

THERE ARE RISKS AND COSTS TO A PROGRAM OF ACTION.
BUT THEY ARE FAR LESS THAN THE LONG-RANGE RISKS
AND COSTS OF COMFORTABLE INACTION.

(John F. Kennedy)

Whatever a man sows, that he will also reap.
And let us not grow weary while doing good, for in due season we shall reap if we do not lose heart.
Therefore, as we have opportunity, let us do good to all, especially to those who are of the household of faith.
(Galatians 6:7, 9-10)

The Last Lap

THERE IS ONLY ONE WAY to get to the finish line...keep running! By 7:00 p.m., October 20, 1968, at the Mexico City Olympics Stadium, it was beginning to darken, it had cooled down. The last of the Olympic marathon runners were being assisted to first-aid stations. Over an hour earlier, Mamo Waldi of Ethiopia had charged across the finish line, winning the 26 mile, 385 yard race looking as strong and as vigorous as when he started. As the last few thousand spectators began to leave, they heard police sirens and whistles entering through the gate to the stadium.

As attention of the remaining crowd turned to the gate, a lone figure wearing the colors of Tanzania came limping pathetically into the stadium. His name was John Steven Aquari. He was the last man to finish this marathon. His leg was bandaged and blood was oozing down his leg. He had taken a bad fall early in the race. Now, it was all he could do to limp his way around the track for that final lap. It was painful to watch. The crowd stood and applauded as he completed that last lap! When he finally crossed the finish line, one of the media reporters asked the question that all of the crowd was thinking: "You are badly injured. Why didn't you quit? Why didn't you give up?"

Aquari, with quiet dignity, spoke volumes: "My country did not send me 7,000 miles to start this race. My country sent me to finish!"

Why is the ending so important? Because it's how a life, a job, a family, a father, or a relationship ends that defines and colors all that has gone on before.

Do you remember Fran Tarkenton? He was the most prolific passer in NFL history. He threw for more yards (until Dan Marino set a new record), scored more touchdowns, ran for more yards than any quarterback in football history. How is he remembered? As a good quarterback but more as a loser type because the Minnesota Vikings lost each time he quarterbacked them to Super Bowl losses. Contrast that to John Elway,

who will be remembered as probably the finest all-around quarterback ever, because he was able to go out in a blaze of glory…winning two Super Bowl championships! The start in life is good…but Dad, you will most likely be remembered by how you finished! Life is not a sprint, it's a marathon!

My prayer and hope for you is that, one of these days, when you cross your finish line, that you, too, along with Paul the Apostle, will be able to shout:
I HAVE FOUGHT THE GOOD FIGHT!
I HAVE FINISHED THE RACE…
I HAVE KEPT THE FAITH!

NOW may the God of peace who brought up our Lord Jesus from the dead, that great Shepherd of the sheep, through the blood of the everlasting covenant, Make you complete in every good work to do His will, working in you what is well pleasing in His sight, through Jesus Christ, to whom be glory forever and ever.
AMEN!
(Hebrews 13:20-21)